STRATEGIC MOVES

Myron K. Leach

STRATEGIC MOVES

Myron K. Leach

Scripture quotations are from Amplified Bible Copyright © 2015 by The Lockman Foundation, La Habra, CA 90631. All rights reserved. NEW INTERNATIONAL VERSION®, NIV® Copyright © 1973, 1978, 1984, 2011 by Biblica, Inc.® Used by permission. All rights reserved worldwide. The King James Version is public domain in the United States. Scripture taken from the New King James Version®. Copyright © 1982 by Thomas Nelson. Used by permission. All rights reserved. Scripture taken from The Message. Copyright © 1993, 1994, 1995, 1996, 2000, 2001, 2002. Used by permission of NavPress Publishing Group.

Published by Harrod Publishing
www.harrodpublishing.com
(240) 244-6082

Printed in the United States
Library of Congress
Harrod Publishing

STRATEGIC MOVES
MYRON K. LEACH

ISBN: 978-0998-8809-90

STRATEGIC MOVES

Myron K. Leach

Published by Harrod Publishing
www.harrodpublishing.com
(240) 244-6082

Printed in the United States
Library of Congress
Harrod Publishing

STRATEGIC MOVES
MYRON K. LEACH

ISBN: 978-0998-8809-90

TABLE OF CONTENTS

ACKNOWLEDGEMENTS

I give God all the glory and honor for the opportunity to share insights that I have gained from various experiences as well as lessons I have gleaned from others. There are many people who have pushed me into my purpose as a man of God, husband and father. I would like to acknowledge my wife, Cynthia who is my best friend, confidant and lover. You are my greatest supporter and I love you for everything you do to build our family and ministry.

To my first born Moriah, AKA #1 who is beautiful inside out and is considered to be my twin in many ways! I thank God for your creative and artistic mind and everything that you do to support me in ministry. I am proud of the woman of God you are becoming!

To my baby Makayla, AKA #2 who is gifted, artistic and unpredictable! Continue to allow the anointing of God to grow in you. He is going to use you to bring many into the kingdom of God. I look forward to what God has in store for you.

In honor of my parents, the late Rev. William Leach and my mother, Annie L. Leach who are in the presence of the Lord. Thank you for a rich inheritance that has been passed to me. I am who I am today because of the seeds that were planted into my life and are now flourishing.

To my biological brothers, Avatus, Anthony (Tony), Darnell, and Gary (Teddy).

I also honor my father and mother in-law, Deacon Clinton D. Venable who has imparted natural and spiritual wisdom to me and the loving late Sadie

M. Venable. To my second family, Deacon Ronald Cash, Rev. Dr. Christine Cash, Rhonda and Longena Cash.

To many who have influence my spiritual journey, my spiritual parents, Bishop Darnell Leach and Dr. Anita Leach. Thank you for teaching me the way of holiness and living a consecrated life. Thank you for taking care of me and allowing me to grow. Thank you for trusting me with the appointment to the ministry you birthed, Shiloh Abundant Life Center - Forestville.

To members of The Oak Grove Missionary Baptist Church of Grayton, MD past and present. To the late Rev. Dr. Edgar L. Williams; Rev. Willis L. Wall; Rev. Yancey Warren; Rev. Avra Jones; Rev. Rodney Young; Rev. Dr. David Durham; Rev. Earl Britt; Bishop Carroll Baltimore; Bishop Richard Scott; the late Dr. Geraldine McInnis; the late Pastors Janice and Robert Baker, the late Pastor William Logan; Bishop Anita O'Brien and Pastor Sandra Sherwood.

To some of my college instructors of Washington Bible College, Pastor Steve Layne, Dr. Carl Sanders. To my close ministry colleagues, Lead Pastor Darrell Reddix, Bishop Timothy Warren, Sr., Pastor Billy T. Staton, Pastor Adam C. Ford, Pastor Clifton Doughty, Sr. and Pastor Deborah Page. The Pastors of the New Beginnings Fellowship. To the Presbytery Board of Shiloh Abundant Life Center - Forestville, I love each of you for your support! I would also like to acknowledge John Lesniewski for being a great business mentor.

To the greatest congregation in the world, Shiloh Abundant Life Center - Forestville. Thank you for giving me the opportunity to serve you and I look forward to the future while building upon a solid foundation

STRATEGIC MOVES: FROM FAILURE TO SUCCESS

INTRODUCTION

I already know what you are thinking and this book is not about chess! It is about making a concerted effort towards back to a stable place and recovering from events that have occurred in your life. Believe it or not, your life has an established order! You may believe in God as I do or you may be an atheist who does not believe in a higher power. I am convinced that what we achieve in life is dependent on God as well as being motivated. The lack of motivation can also be a dream killer and it would be unfortunate to allow your dreams to die and never pursue them.

This book is all about taking action, moving from laziness and doing exactly what you are supposed to do! Yes, I am preaching to the choir because it took me several years to realize what was already inside of me. God has pushed me to share my insights of how to strategically move from neutral to taking action. God has propelled me into the present and everything that I am destined to achieve in my future.

As I prepared to write this book, I immediately thought about the game of chess. I was always intrigued by the board set up and the significance of each game piece. I have discovered that there are rules that you should know before playing the game. You must always *protect* the king because the king has infinite value; don't be *careless* in wasting any of your game pieces by making a wrong move. *Control* the center of the game board, and *use all* of the board pieces. These areas are significant to each area of one's life and this prompts us to be strategic at every juncture in life. I will talk about these areas in greater detail throughout this book.

Everyone has a future but it is tied into how we use our time, talents and resources to overcome potential obstacles and learn from our life lessons. Life lessons are often the most difficult because we usually don't see it coming. It can be an unexpected health challenge, changes in relationships, financial difficulties, or death of a loved one.

We must realize that we have the ability to be strategic in our relationships, personal goals and ambitions, music or art, as well as dreams. What has stopped you from moving forward? Has the opinions of people caused you to not move forward and realize your God-given potential?

You may be one who has made an attempt at trying something new or thought you could obtain something within your grasp or tried something and failed. I have good news for you! You can strategically achieve the dreams that are in your heart and mind to bring it to fruition.

As a child growing up, a label was placed upon me in elementary school. I was like many of my friends who was energetic, curious, and talkative. This behavior got me into trouble and some of my teachers had a negative view of me. Unfortunately, I embraced their assessment. I had to overcome the stigma of being a bad kid, instead I was actually gifted!

STRATEGIC MOVES: FROM FAILURE TO SUCCESS

INTRODUCTION

I already know what you are thinking and this book is not about chess! It is about making a concerted effort towards back to a stable place and recovering from events that have occurred in your life. Believe it or not, your life has an established order! You may believe in God as I do or you may be an atheist who does not believe in a higher power. I am convinced that what we achieve in life is dependent on God as well as being motivated. The lack of motivation can also be a dream killer and it would be unfortunate to allow your dreams to die and never pursue them.

This book is all about taking action, moving from laziness and doing exactly what you are supposed to do! Yes, I am preaching to the choir because it took me several years to realize what was already inside of me. God has pushed me to share my insights of how to strategically move from neutral to taking action. God has propelled me into the present and everything that I am destined to achieve in my future.

As I prepared to write this book, I immediately thought about the game of chess. I was always intrigued by the board set up and the significance of each game piece. I have discovered that there are rules that you should know before playing the game. You must always *protect* the king because the king has infinite value; don't be *careless* in wasting any of your game pieces by making a wrong move. *Control* the center of the game board, and *use all* of the board pieces. These areas are significant to each area of one's life and this prompts us to be strategic at every juncture in life. I will talk about these areas in greater detail throughout this book.

Everyone has a future but it is tied into how we use our time, talents and resources to overcome potential obstacles and learn from our life lessons. Life lessons are often the most difficult because we usually don't see it coming. It can be an unexpected health challenge, changes in relationships, financial difficulties, or death of a loved one.

We must realize that we have the ability to be strategic in our relationships, personal goals and ambitions, music or art, as well as dreams. What has stopped you from moving forward? Has the opinions of people caused you to not move forward and realize your God-given potential?

You may be one who has made an attempt at trying something new or thought you could obtain something within your grasp or tried something and failed. I have good news for you! You can strategically achieve the dreams that are in your heart and mind to bring it to fruition.

As a child growing up, a label was placed upon me in elementary school. I was like many of my friends who was energetic, curious, and talkative. This behavior got me into trouble and some of my teachers had a negative view of me. Unfortunately, I embraced their assessment. I had to overcome the stigma of being a bad kid, instead I was actually gifted!

On another note, I believe our public school systems are ill equipped to address children who might have attention deficits and may be gifted in many areas! A gift existed within me which was artistic and creative but had to be cultivated over time. The cultivation process can be long and arduous but will yield great results if given proper attention.

We must give attention to things that are profitable to our lives which will allow us to fulfill our purpose. We are born with purpose but we have to strategically work the plan! We must constantly take inventory of our lives and utilize what works for us and replace other things that are not profitable.

Fast forward, I have strategically moved forward with the assistance of many people in my life. My father and mother were very instrumental in facilitating my creative, artistic, and musical ability. They allowed me to grow into who I am today with prayer, patience, and guidance. They strategically permitted me to bloom through my adolescent years into adulthood.

As a parent, entrepreneur, and pastor, I now have the same responsibility to guide, encourage, correct, and give those who are connected to me the strategic tools that will help them mature into Godly individuals as well as helping them to grow in every area of life.

We must be strategic about everything that concerns our lives. Taking everything for granted can cause you to not fulfill your purpose if you are not careful. Therefore, I invite you to go with me on this journey to make strategic moves for your life!

CHAPTER 1

MAKING WISE DECISIONS

"Now the Lord said to Joshua, "Do not fear or be dismayed (intimidated). Take all the men of war with you and set out, go up to Ai; see, I have given the king of Ai, his people, his city, and his land into your hand." Joshua 8:1 (AMP)

Life is often filled with moments that dictate our future. Every step that we take has the potential to set us back or thrust us into the future. Just as Joshua was faced with decisions and fears, we must count the costs and be aware of little things that we must deal with. Ai was a small location in the Bible that was designed by God to be easily conquered. Unfortunately, it ended up being one of the worst defeats for the nation of Israel.

As I mentioned in the introduction, you must protect the king; and, I would add to protect the King inside of you. You have immeasurable worth that should not be wasted. The King of time and talent controls your destiny and how you allow others to utilize it. You cannot give everything to everyone, but you should find people to invest your life into.

One of the greatest leadership lessons I have learned is to pour into others what I have gleaned from those who have mentored me. Everyone has an obligation to reciprocate their life lessons to those who are connected to them through family relationships, business, and within our congregations. I believe every relationship has strategic purposes with some strategic purposes lasting for a season and others lasting for a lifetime. Ultimately, we will be held accountable with our time.

Paying attention to details and proper instructions can bring success or it can result in a crushing defeat. Putting together furniture or an accessory can be challenging if you don't follow instructions. The lack of missing components or damaging a vital piece of furniture can cause misfortune as well. This tells me that one should take caution when embarking in various endeavors.

Joshua did not fully heed the Word that was spoken by God and became overconfident. They were in the right position to win but failed to consult God. I must also add that Joshua had to deal with internal issues in the camp. These issues seemed small but had a great impact on the entire nation of Israel.

Many times we have to deal with things that are minuscule but God wants us to take inventory. We must take inventory of our motives and anything that is not holy. Yes I said holy! These things are sacred to God and before we can achieve total victory, we must be honest with God and ourselves. We must put ourselves in the right position!

Making wise decisions is a key step to obtaining victory in your life, business, and work life. Making wise decisions help us to make the right moves and not be hasty in our behavior. While working on this project, I was listening to a radio program and was struck by the on air conversation. A caller's statement has stuck with me until this day which was "we must constantly think about the end in mind while not becoming stuck in what we see but look forward by faith and foresight."

Working with the end in mind is difficult for some because of the need for immediate gratification; but, we must be mindful about our lives and how we will get to the end of what we are working towards.

Having a strategy for every area of your life will bring success. Having a strategy will ensure that when difficulties come, you will not lose your mind or your faith. One of the mistakes that I made early in my business career was not preparing for a drought. Yes, I thought I would always be rolling in the dough but a recession hit during 2007 and it affected me in ways I did not prepare for. I failed to see the end by not paying attention to the small details.

Things that seem miniscule can have dire effects on one's life. *"Catch for us the foxes, the little foxes that ruin the vineyards, our vineyards that are in bloom."* Song of Songs 2:15 (NIV). I eventually learned the hard lesson that if I wanted to succeed again, I would have to make changes to my business practices, my manner of thinking, and pay attention to detail. It has been a long road back to what I would deem as normal and I have learned lessons that will allow me to succeed in life and in ministry.

You can experience success after failure! It may be hard but your season can change if you are strategic and make wise decisions. Making wise decisions means that you are willing to change. I had to learn how to think differently about God, myself, and my destiny. I had to learn to adapt to change by overcoming fear and intimidation.

3

When you properly address your inner feelings, you can face the giant situation with transformative thinking. Transformative thinking is mixed with faith and self-determination that you can adapt to recover from anything.

I had to strategically think about my future and put a plan of action into place. After trying many things that I thought would be a remedy, I was placed into a strategic position that allowed me to put my business expertise into action.

I was strategically given an opportunity to join an associate to provide professional services in the area of real estate. I could have not accepted this opportunity due to insecurities but this was my chance to get back to a place of stability.

All it takes is one God-ordained opportunity to change the course of your future. God can use people, places, and situations to get you back on track. Was it divine intervention for me? Yes, because God knew that I learned the lesson for that season of my life and I would not have to repeat it!

When you make wise decisions, God will set things in motion but it is based upon your drive to succeed. Failure is never final but it may feel that it is. Failure can bring success if the lesson is learned and this is normally verified by your conduct.

He will bring things together that will cause you to know that it is His hand at work. What are you asking God to do for you? What steps are your taking and do you believe that you can achieve what is in your heart?

The seventh chapter of Joshua is filled with biblical techniques and provides specific instructions of how to get back on track. You can get back on track by listening to the Holy Spirit, having discernment, and devoting yourselves to God. I believe the Holy Spirit guides us strategically in a direction that will take us to our destination points.

Destination points are markers that force us to move forward. They are often painful but they are beneficial. Destination points teach us lessons of how to respond to our situations and remain focused on what is ahead. Destination points also heighten our spiritual discernment. Just in case you don't know what spiritual discernment is, it is the ability to judge well. For Christians, it is often used for spiritual direction.

Our discernment will prompt us to perceive the motives of people and their motivation. Everyone is not motivated to do the right thing and may be assigned to your life to take you off your course. We must have discernment which will allow us to see people for who they are and determine if they are a healthy influence or unhealthy hindrance. If certain individuals are not beneficial to your life, it would be in your best interest to evict them from your life.

Destination points allow you to perceive what is working and what is not beneficial. I also believe they allow you to be introspective. When one examines their life truthfully, they will be forced to look at good and negative qualities. We should give special attention to our negative qualities and allow them to be reshaped so we can utilize those areas as strategic strength.

5

When you wholly devote your life to God, you will come into spiritual alignment with His will. God's *will* is based upon our cooperation, determination and discernment. This equals devotion to God!

It is possible to get off track by thinking you are self-sufficient. I can attest that this is one of the greatest mistakes that anyone can make. We must make wise decisions by listening to wise counsel. *"Where no counsel is, the people fall: but in the multitude of counsellors there is safety."* Proverbs 11:14 (KJV).

Wise decisions provide a roadmap towards victory. God has a strategy for our victory and we must constantly ask Him for guidance. It is also important to listen to wise counsel of those who are spiritual. Everyone should have at least one person to hold them accountable. Accountability allows one to shed unnecessary clutter and baggage that can hinder their future.

Wise decisions allow you to execute the plan of action. We must discern when to stand still and when to pursue. When we properly execute the plan, one can accomplish everything that God has destined for their life. Make decisions that will save your life and those who are connected to you.

Making a wise decision can be uncomfortable because it goes against what is comfortable. I believe if you are too comfortable, you may not be growing. Wisdom often comes after trials and difficulties. As I have previously mentioned, I grew in wisdom after losing just about everything. Wisdom will teach you what to do and what not to do in the future!

6

Action Plan:

1. What areas do you need to make better decisions?

2. What do you need to do differently regarding past failures?

3. Do you have a plan of action?

4. What are your next steps?

CHAPTER 2

WORKING TOWARD THE GOAL

"I'm not saying that I have this all together, that I have it made. But I am well on my way, reaching out for Christ, who has so wondrously reached out for me. Friends, don't get me wrong: By no means do I count myself an expert in all of this, but I've got my eye on the goal, where God is beckoning us onward—to Jesus. I'm off and running, and I'm not turning back." Philippians 3:12-14 (MSG)

Like most people, I hate to get lost and don't like to ask for directions. I also have noticed that if you have a GPS system, it can direct you along a route that may be out of the way or unfamiliar. I have learned that it is okay to ask for help especially if you are having difficulty. God wants to help us in our journey and we must learn how to ask Him. *"Ask and it will be given to you; seek and you will find; knock and the door will be opened to you."* Matthew 7:7 (NIV)

Working towards your goal will require you to not waste anything of value and use every resource to its maximum value. I mentioned earlier that in the game of chess, one cannot be careless with their game pieces in making the wrong move.

I had to learn this lesson the hard way because I wasted time and money on the wrong thing in my late 20's. I did not value money and spent it as fast as I made it! I squandered my game pieces, which symbolizes money, for things that looked good but did not have lasting value.

My advice to anyone who is in their 20's to spend wisely and save for the future because you will not stay young! My mom took note of some of my spending habits and prompted me to make some changes. I did not immediately listen to her and fell deeper into the trap of credit card debt.

I had to dig myself out of a deep hole with the guidance of a debt counselor and legal assistance. Was it embarrassing? Yes it was but I had learned how to use my game pieces correctly.

You see, after you have failed a few times, it should teach you something correctly. You should learn to do things the right way at the right time and to delay instant gratification. Don't allow your pride to hold you back from making decisions that will thrust you forward.

Many times we also fail to seek assistance from those we are connected to such as family, colleagues, mentors or unconventional means. Some people think the universe directs and places things in order but I believe that there is a higher power through the power of Jesus Christ. It is His power that operates in us that gives us the ability to be active, engaged, and strategically work towards our goals.

The mistake that some people make is the belief that God will do everything. While it is true that He can do anything, He gives us the physical and mental fortitude to achieve and complete what is inside of us. We must give life to our dreams and be major contributors to our goals. We have to put ourselves in the right position, at the right time and place as well as strategic partnerships.

9

You must deal with internal landmines. One of the most difficult landmines is overcoming laziness and a lack of motivation. You must tap into your inner strength to counter these behaviors which may be innate or what you were predisposed and dig deep to bring out positive and healthy habits.

One of the most difficult things is starting a project or personal goal and maintaining focus to complete it. For example, you may be one who would like to lose weight or you would like to lower a dosage of medicine prescribed by your doctor for a specified condition. You must fight the enemy within to start, overcome fear, and be accountable to the goal.

Accountability can be difficult for some because of the "lone ranger syndrome." This syndrome is self-centered and causes one to exclude assistance and help that will allow you to win or complete your goal.

Accountability is a great thing when utilized correctly and is healthy in many ways. It causes you to realize that you cannot do somethings by yourself. Being accountable allows you to see things from another perspective and limits your liability. Everyone should have at least one accountability relationship. It is a safety net which will allow you to maneuver through difficult seasons of life as well as celebrate accomplishments.

Working towards a goal requires one to be prepared. Preparation takes work and intentional fortitude. It also requires one to deal with divine interruptions. I will admit, some interruptions are not divine but are self-inflicted. If you are not careful, there is the potential to sabotage your future.

Working toward your goals requires direction, discipline, correct vision and faith. I had to correct each of these areas as I prepared for my pastoral assignment. I had to go through a season of preparing while serving for an assignment that I had doubts about. Yes, I knew I was called and it was even prophesied that I would be a pastor one day, but I had to work towards my aspirations and deal with internal landmines.

These landmines usually are attached to how others view you and their lack of confidence and trust. If you are a leader in any capacity, you know what I am talking about. You must learn how to work in your area of assignment while trying to overcome the glass ceiling. The glass ceiling that others have place over us can affect your thinking and cause you to doubt your own abilities if you are not careful.

You will also have to overcome external landmines which may or may not be visible. You can overcome external landmines by being focused on your life, ministry and work assignments. You should be focused on the positives and less focused on negative thoughts.

You must be dedicated to growing internally which will affect how you deal with external factors. The good news is that you already have the grace and the ability to overcome internal and external landmines!

11

My landmines taught me valuable lessons of how to work through difficult things. Life threw me a curveball as a worked towards my personal goal of obtaining my bachelor's degree. My mom became ill and went home to be with Lord in 2003. I had just decided to go back to school, and completed a successful academic year and I looked forward to completing my degree in just a few years.

After my mom passed, I decided that I would forego a few semesters and deal with my own grief. There will be seasons of your life when you have to take time to refocus and reset. This is not to say that you can't grieve and complete goals and accomplishments. You have to know yourself and your limitations and constantly set goals for your life. Goal setting is imperative to staying true to yourself and the path of life that has been laid out for you.

There will be seasons in your life when you will have to deal with external and internal issues while working towards your goals. I had to bear down and go through a hard process that allowed me to heal but also developed perseverance.

If you work in any area of ministry or a secular job, you are still expected to plow through and fulfill your obligations. Working towards your goal means that you may have roadblocks and distractions but you must continue.

You must continue through the messiness of life and depend on the Holy Spirit. If you are a believer in Jesus Christ, you will realize that you have access to the greatest power available to mankind. When you truly rely on the Holy Spirit, you will be able to thrive even when you are at your lowest point.

As I prepared for pastoral ministry, I became aware of negative behavioral responses of some of my ministry colleagues. I began to notice that many people developed the habit of stopping and not completing assignments due to internal and external life-events. I observed many individuals who allowed their circumstances to overwhelm them to the point of not functioning or quitting for various reasons.

I believe roadblocks and distractions should not cause us to become discontent with God but should cause us to grow closer to Him. While we may not understand His ways and His timing, we must be determined to stay committed to our work and go through.

I am not being insensitive to anyone's situation, but I just believe that you must find a way to endure. Enduring does not mean that your experiences are not important, but it means that you will find ways to keep going no matter what. To endure means to forge through events because time and life does not stop!

There are events that will cause you to come to a standstill, but you must learn how to navigate through the tough stuff, remain focused and keep living your life. Navigating through these situations may dictate the need to join a support group, obtain therapeutic assistance and finding new methods to direct your energy.

There have been several events that have affected my life and my immediate family. My wife and I experienced the loss of employment simultaneously which in turn affected us economically. We nearly lost everything; but in the midst of what we were experiencing, we made a determination to remain faithful to each other and our ministry assignments while going through challenging times.

Our challenging season forced us to be strategically aligned spiritually with God and each other. There were times when we literally wanted to give up but we knew that giving up was not an option! As a result of these events, God allowed us to be a reflection of His restoring power.

You must be resolute even when the walls of life are closing in, and you must know that you will come out better because God will give you strength to persevere. Perseverance is an inner force that will allow you to climb out of a deep emotional valley and make it to a place that is safe. It is a survival zone that will allow you to find God at your lowest point while abiding in His presence.

The survival zone will allow you to get your footing and obtain stability. This place will also allow you to navigate through seasons of isolation. Isolation is often viewed in a negative manner because it often secludes us from human interaction. There are positives and negatives to isolation and one must tactically use this human emotion wisely.

Negative aspects of isolation includes brooding over mistakes, not allowing others to assist you in your time of distress and the separation from God. I had firsthand experience in each of these areas and had to find a way to fight through the convenience of this

14

emotional plight. Positive aspects of isolation are developing spiritual and mental toughness, growing spiritually and gaining a new perspective.

There was an event that affected my family that occurred during the early hours before a Resurrection Sunday morning. No one in our family anticipated the events that would occur that morning. Needless to say, we were emotionally and physically drained and could have chosen to check out and just stay at home to tend to our wounds; but, we persevered with the help of the Lord. Each of us were able to fulfill our obligations to the congregation that we serve and the Lord provided comfort and strength for our assignments.

I believe God gives us the fortitude to press forward despite domestic difficulties that may cause us to get off course. There will be seasons when you have to withdraw to heal emotionally, rest physically and obtain proper counsel. These aspects will help you to be effective and be a source of inspiration to others.

If you get off course, dig deep within yourself and strategically get back into the race. Your race course may include many turns, hills and slopes but you must find a way to traverse each segment. We must endure every season of life that we experience.

You must endure to get to your expected end. You must be able to navigate clear and present dangers that are obvious. Endurance will develop your vision and will aid you to identify attacks of the enemy, as well as knowing how to respond while in your storm.

There will be seasons when you will be discontented and may be intimidated by what you see.

This is where your faith should kick in and cause you to rely upon it. The worst decision that you could make is to derail your future based on something that you may not comprehend in the natural. We must learn to view things spiritually and seek guidance from God to deal with those experiences.

Working toward your goals will involve failure. I did not realize it at the time but my failures prepared me for my future. This can be difficult for most because no one likes to fail. Failure has the potential to cause you to be paralyzed by fear, rejection and embarrassment.

You must realize that failure is never final or fatal. God has a strategy for our victory and we must learn lessons along the way that will push us forward. Let your failures fuel you beyond what you have experienced. Allow your failures to motivate you to achieving your dreams and fulfill your purpose.

You have to use your God-given resources while giving attention to areas that are deficient. Deficient areas don't have to disqualify you from making proper moves, but it is important to work on imperfect areas by learning techniques, studying those who have a successful track record and learn how to recalibrate.

Recalibrating allows you to do something over and to go in a new or the intended direction. I had to learn how to recalibrate while recovering from a series of bad decisions. You may have goals that you wish to achieve; but, learn how to pace yourself. Recalibrating allows you to get rid of excessive baggage and clutter.

There will be times when you have to think differently about where you want to go and where you want to be.

You must rid yourself of unnecessary weights while working with a strategic mindset. It is about getting in step with God and not talking yourself out of your destination because it appears too difficult. What are you carrying that is not fruitful and necessary?

Recalibrating allows one to accomplish extraordinary things but it's according to our connection. Your connection with God will allow you to draw strength during the most difficult events in your life.

When you recalibrate, it allows you to reposition yourself and take proper action. Pursue your dreams and don't stop until you obtain it. You may have to take a few detours, but get back on track because your future is waiting for you!

You must have a resolve to keep going despite potential hindrances. Just because an interruption arises, does not mean you have to stop in your tracks. Keep running and don't stop until you have crossed the finish line.

As I prepared for this manuscript, a social media clip about two ladies racing caught my attention. There were two ladies who were at the point of crossing the finish line but they failed to take note of one who was behind them. This individual paced her lap in a manner that allowed her to catch up with the two leaders and she won the race! Her pace may have seemed slow in the beginning but she utilized a strategy to overcome the crowd, maintain her composure, used her energy wisely and sustained good vision.

While you are pursing your goal and dreams, you will have to overcome the opinions of the crowd. There will be some who will support you and give you accolades. Others may exhibit distrust in your abilities and unfair comparisons. This is the time to be confident in your own ability and perfect it.

You must learn to maintain your composure in seasons of testing and proving. It is not the fact that you are attempting to prove something to others but you are developing into who God called you to be.

Using your energy correctly can yield lifetime benefits. If you pace yourself and not attempt to do too much at one time, you will be able to operate at your optimum level in your family, business and ministry assignments. You must learn to temper your emotions and not get caught up in a whirlwind of excitement.

Maintaining good vision is necessary because what you see may not be what you expect. This is when you must allow your faith to arise and rely upon your inner instincts and discernment. Everyone has a race to run so run your race as the Lord leads!

ACTION PLAN:

1. Identify what got you off track.

2. Don't delay your responses to things that require your immediate attention.

3. Be calculating and thoughtful about how to move forward.

4. Have a plan of accountability and be accountable to a life coach, mentor, pastor or a counselor.

5. Recalibrate, rest, think, plan, prepare!

CHAPTER 3

OVERCOMING DISCONTENTMENT AND INTIMIDATION

"I am not saying this because I am in need, for I have learned to be content whatever the circumstances." Philippians 4:11 (NIV)

You cannot have success without dealing with discontentment and intimidation. These areas can be redirected to become stepping blocks to achievement. Discontentment does not mean that you must settle for less than what you expect, but should drive you towards what is in your heart and what you have planned. Discontentment almost stopped me from obtaining my Master's degree because I was dissatisfied with my life and began to compare my life against some of my associates' achievements. Despite my inner struggles, there was something that allowed me to keep going.

I had to face discontentment of not having enough resources to continue but I had desire. My desire pushed me to start researching what I had to do to get to the next level. I had to push beyond what I viewed as an impossible achievement. I was in my early 40's going to graduate school and was intimidated by what I saw. I almost talked myself out of pursuing my degree because of personal obligations, recovering from the recession and just plain scared!

God allowed me to recover mentally and spiritually and also gave me a strategic plan to complete the degree program. With hard work and perseverance, I was able to complete something that I initially deemed impossible. This period in my life revealed that I had the ability to complete the work and I was competent enough to thrive. God will give you just what you need to complete every task for your life.

I had to overcome the limitations that I placed on myself and press forward. Many times in life, we will have to talk ourselves off of the so called ledge! This ledge can paralyze us to do nothing, but we must remember that there is something great in us. There is a greater purpose that is designed by God. We must conquer the inhabitants of doubt and self-deception. Doubt and self-deception will not leave until we make a strategic move and replace it with hope, faith and determination!

Very early in my musical career, I was intimidated by another musician during a church service. This person was highly gifted and possessed talent that I desired. It was uncomfortable, but it drove me to get better and to develop my God given ability. He was more experienced than I was but we both possessed similar skill.

There will be times when others have the same gift but you must embrace your gift and allow it to be developed. I had a desire to play like him right away, but I later realized perfection requires time. I had to learn the process of embracing, cultivating and using my gift! This process will work in any area of your life that is viewed as deficient.

Overcoming self-doubt and negative emotions requires time. Allow yourself to grow from where you are into who and what God wants you to be. Perfect your gift and craft and when this occurs, you will experience fulfillment as well as those who are connected to you.

Don't allow intimidation to stop you because it may seem too hard. Paying attention to every detail can thrust you beyond your doubts and insecurities. I had to learn how to use the gifts that God gave me and not compare myself to others. We must realize that God has gifted everyone differently.

I had to learn how to control the center of the game board by overcoming my own emotions. We have one life to live and we have to learn how to center ourselves so we can be effective naturally and spiritually. What you do in the natural will affect your spiritual growth and vice a versa. There is a cause and effect to everything that happens.

Perfect what is already within you! Realize the God-given potential that resides in you and all you have to do is tap into it. *"Therefore I remind you to stir up the gift of God which is in you through the laying on of my hands. For God has not given us a spirit of fear, but of power and of love and of a sound mind."* 2 Timothy 1:6-7 (NKJV)

Perfection is a process! If you need evidence and assurance, you will discover it in Psalm 138:8a (KJV) *"The Lord will perfect that which concerns me."* God is with us each step of the way but we have to allow Him to do the work in us while doing our part. Our part involves going through the process that will bring us to a point of completion. Completion is something that brings closure to one thing but prepares you for the next phase.

Use the resources that you have to overcome your current situation. Be willing to enlist help from people. You should consult your pastor, a life coach or counselor, or possibly an attorney to aid you in overcoming barriers. Wherever you are in life or your game board, learn how to get back to the center!

You must learn to pay attention to the signs. There are natural and spiritual signs that are obvious and some not so obvious. I was driving and noticed two individuals attempting to cross a street but their sign was orange which meant they did not have authorization to cross. They paused but proceeded to walk ill-advised. The results of their decision could have ended in a calamity or even death because they broke the rule.

You must know when to move forward, take steps in either direction, move backwards or remain in the same position. Each movement has ramifications -positive or negative, and you must learn to live with those choices as well as making notes for future actions.

How many times have you made an ill-advised decision that ended in failure or something more drastic? In a chess game, the rules mandate before a move is made, a certain set of requirements must be met. Meeting the requirements show you have thought about the movements I previously spoke about and have mapped out an initial strategy. As you think about your life, think about the direction you desire for your life and work the plan! You may have to do things multiple times until you learn the lesson and/or seek direction to achieve a specific goal.

I believe God's will changes our perception when we yield to His guidance. When we surrender to God's will, we obtain the best answer about our questions. As you go through things in life, don't focus on the issues but ask God for a sign when you don't understand what you are going through. As you strategically pray, God will reveal things to you. He will reveal His divine plan of action for you but you must be engaged.

Being engaged requires you to wait for an answer. Waiting is difficult for most people because we live in an instant gratification culture. When we are willing to wait, we will gain revelation, obtain strength, and it will counter any fears.

While you wait, you will also gain confirmation to move forward, move in a specific direction or standstill. You must also be careful not to over-analyze your situation and entertain analysis paralysis. This is the inability to move in any direction. You must come to a place in your life when you have taken proper steps to move strategically.

Most people need proof before they will believe in something. Intimidation can delay your progress or it can push you into your future. Instead of giving in to discontentment and intimidation, redirect your energy to build confidence that God will give you peace and confirm His presence.

Action Plan:

1. Take time to reflect on areas of discontentment and devise a plan to move forward.

2. Embrace your natural and spiritual gifts. Pay attention to internal and external signs.

3. Delay your instant gratification.

CHAPTER 4

ADAPTING TO CHANGE

"For as he thinks in his heart, so is he." Proverbs 23:7a (NKJV)

Change is often painful and uncomfortable. Change can also be irritating and is often rejected by people. Change can be healthy and will often alter the trajectory of your life if you learn to adapt.

Adapting to change requires you to be fully aware. You must know yourself and how to navigate through spiritual attacks. The ability to be victorious begins with how you think. Your thought process can affect your reality in ways that can keep you stuck in the past.

We must embrace the past as events that have molded us into who are. Adapting to change requires us to reframe our thinking about ourselves and the situation.

I was engaged in a conversation with a member of our congregation and they shared with me how God was allowing them to go through a long process of healing. They indicated that they were being reframed and how their outlook on life was changing. This individual was learning how to live in their new normal. Getting to this point is often difficult because it involves emotions and it involves a process of changing one's mindset.

You cannot go into any battle with an attitude of defeat. Things may seem overwhelming but you must find a way to win. The odds may be stacked against you but find a way to flip the script.

You must strategize to come out on top. This does not have to be at the expense of others, but you must be sober minded. When you think strategically, God will give you a plan. He will give you a plan of action to get to the next place in your life.

When you adapt to change, your entire outlook will change! Most of us are creatures of habit, but it's good to change things up a bit so you won't get stuck in a rut. Technology forces us to change because there are new ideas flooding our society every day. We may not realize it but change has to occur to make us grow!

You may be reading this book and having trouble adjusting to your new normal. Your new normal could be the result of the death of a loved one, divorce, financial challenges, health issues, or making an attempt to find your way. You can begin again, recover, and reset your life. It all begins with your heart and your mind being God-centered as well as taking the necessary steps to adapt.

Adapt by finding new methods for something that used to work that is not currently working well. Your life is similar to a home that was built several years ago. Everything was good at that time, but it may need to be renovated! Renovation is simply the means to bring back into a like new state of being or better than the original state. Be willing to remove the old stuff and make room for the new and improved you!

27

Adapting to change will be your ally if you allow it to take root in your life without resisting the change of direction!

ACTION PLAN:

1. Adapt to change by taking small steps!

2. Adapt to change by adopting new methods!

3. Develop the right attitude even when things are difficult.

CHAPTER 5

BREAKING A LOSING SEASON

Isaac reopened the wells that had been dug in the time of his father Abraham, which the Philistines had stopped up after Abraham died, and he gave them the same names his father had given them. Gen. 26:18 (NIV)

Overcoming losing seasons in your life will require consistency and faith to persevere. Isaac could have stopped digging wells to find new water sources but the Bible reveals the mindset of Isaac and how to face opposition by not stopping.

Isaac learned lessons along the way as he lived through the famine in Genesis 26. Living through losing seasons will cause you to have a mindset of giving up or finding a way to move forward. The key is living through your seasons of drought. Isaac chose to keep going despite opposition. Every time he faced opposition, he dug another well. Don't stop digging!

The game of chess teaches you how to handle losing while learning. You will become a better player by repetition and learning the function of each game piece. The premise is to become better. You have to keep playing the game! You have to learn how to deal with losing seasons in your life to build endurance. You must learn to make necessary adjustments and discern when trouble may be ahead.

I am an avid sports fan and I have observed teams that have established winning traditions and those who are often the bottom feeders in their perspective leagues. I noted that the habits of many teams displayed an attitude of doing what it takes to get better. I also watched other athletes who were willing to participate in off-season training while others avoid it at all cost even when there was an incentive to take part. I also noted coaches doing extra work to gain a competitive edge.

Gaining a competitive edge requires you to do what another person is not willing to do even if they have the same opportunity to improve. What are you doing to improve your life and current circumstances? Are you willing to put in the extra work?

A losing mindset conditions you to believe you cannot grow and make improvements. This type of mindset is usually missing a sense of hope. I am here today because I had hope! There was an inner drive to keep going while wanting to give up. This may sound crazy but I knew if I wanted to get to my desired destination, I had to change my state of mind.

When you begin to sow into areas that you want to see grow, you will begin to see increase! This applies to natural as well as spiritual things. If you have a desire to increase the bottom line in your business or ministry, you have to take inventory of everything that you have as well as what you don't possess and put in the work! You must cultivate your resources and allow them to work for you. You may be thinking that you don't have enough. Start where you are and work with what you have.

I want to share my experience of tithing to my local church. I had resources and I had a desire, but my faith was limited in my early years as a believer in Jesus Christ. I decided to give a level that I deemed was comfortable but I later discovered that level was not my best.

I discovered that tithing was not just a part of the worship service, but it was the way I would break my losing season. I had resources but I was not being honest with myself or to God. Early in my marriage, I made the decision that our household would be tithers to our local church. Was this a difficult decision? The answer is yes! But I wanted to give God the best of me so that I could position my family to new levels of favor. I also had to learn the value of being a gross tither versus being a net tither!

You may be asking yourself how I came to this conclusion. Well, it was a process and did not happen overnight. I am not trying to upset your applecart, but I believe that giving is an act of worship that unties the hands of God. I encourage you to examine your heart and take the necessary steps to give a tithe of your income. You may be saying that you cannot afford to tithe and this may be true. I would encourage you to give an acceptable offering that allows you to develop good giving habits.

If you want to see financial increase, begin to sow a seed and develop a tithing lifestyle! I believe in the principle of tithing and this principle also applies in giving of your time, resources and talents.

Growing in this practice of giving came with much difficulty because I had to dig myself out of a mountain of debt. However, I was determined to give God my best by honoring Him with what I earned. Over time, I developed a mindset of giving what I had and God has blessed me to this day because I had a desire to give. When you have a desire, God will honor your heart. I can attest that I literally gave my way out of a losing season!

I attended a conference several years ago and learned a valuable technique from Pastor John K. Jenkins who is the Pastor of the First Baptist Church of Glenarden, MD. He encouraged us to put into practice a technique called "Critical Standards and Vital Signs." He indicated that this practice has allowed each area in their ministry to evaluate what is working well, measure it against things that were not working or flowing properly, and to evaluate the necessary steps to find solutions to what needed to change or improve.

This technique sounded somewhat complicated, but it forced me to think critically about what is not working well in my life and ministry. It allowed me to recall areas in my life that were not as successful as they should have been and take necessary steps to fulfill my dreams and desires.

From that day forward, I constantly ask myself, what is not working and what changes or adjustments do I need to make with the help of the Lord? Utilize the critical standards and vital signs technique for your life and it will force you to look deep within yourself and help you to break the chains of a losing season.

A losing season for you could be overcoming an illness, negative emotions, low self-esteem or a failed business. I'm sure you get the picture by now! Whatever has held you back, you have the ability to make changes and turn things around. You can break the losing cycle by doing the needed things. It will come with much opposition, but make a determination to change your trajectory. You can break your losing season!

ACTION PLAN:

1. Invest in yourself!

2. Commit to the process of change.

3. Be consistent to break old habits by developing new habits for at least 30 days.

4. Develop a system and/or measurements to obtain the better results for specific areas of your life.

CHAPTER 6

OVERCOMING EXCUSES

But Moses said, "Pardon your servant, Lord. Please send someone else." Exodus 4:13 (NIV)

How many times have you been disobedient and came up with an excuse to avoid doing something that was required? Well, Moses was one who had to overcome his limitations and he came up with many excuses of being disobedient to God. The Bible describes him as one who did not speak well, hot-tempered, and had to learn how to delegate duties. He had to also learn how to overcome the opinions of others. He had a lot on his hands, but God saw something that Moses did not see about himself.

Moses had to overcome the fear of rejection and making mistakes. Conquering fear of rejection is a process that occurs over a period of time. Mastering the fear of rejection will occur when you change your view of yourself. You must be comfortable in your own skin and be less prone to compare yourself to others.

Fear and rejection are the enemies to your strategic victory! Fear and rejection are real feelings; however, it does not have to dominate your life! Many are paralyzed by past failures as well as low self-esteem. Failure is actually a great teacher of how to proceed in a specific direction, but it also allows you to change your behavior by re-engaging your energy and not repeating familiar patterns.

We must be aware of things that cause us to be fearful and face them with self-determination. We should face our fears knowing that they do not have to limit our growth. We must allow fear to be a stepping stone above any obstacle that is in front of us with the assurance that we can conquer it.

I had to overcome the excuse of what I deemed as limited resources. Don't limit what you already have by making an excuses. I had to learn that my gift mattered and had to tap into it. We must learn the principle that despite our limitations, we must use what we have. It is easy to become jealous of what someone else has but be confident in your abilities.

Conquering fear means that you may have to revisit the past but do not stay there! The past is often our best teacher and it will force us to face our present realities and move towards our destiny.

Conquering your fear requires time, focus, and re-training your brain. You must make affirmations to yourself as well as being accountable to someone who can help you get over natural and spiritual obstacles. I encourage you to meditate on the Word of God, read helpful books, prayer, and invest in resources that will empower you as well as assist you in overcoming excuses.

Excuses are the easy way out, but we have to ask ourselves is it really the best thing for us? At some point in our life, there has to be a decision to move beyond excuses and limitations. When you learn to overcome your excuses, you will grow!

I have learned that you can function with limitations by not allowing them to diminish your worth and value.

ACTION PLAN:

1. Learn how to conquer your fears with faith and strategies.

2. Don't allow disobedience or excuses stop you from making progress.

3. Use your resources wisely. (Finances, Talents and Time)

CHAPTER 7

WATCH OUT FOR BLIND SPOTS

"Watch and pray so that you will not fall into temptation. The spirit is willing, but the flesh is weak."
Matthew 26:41 (NIV)

Blind spots are areas that are not obvious and are perceived differently by our natural bents and/or worldviews. Sometimes it is difficult to view things from another perspective, but this does not mean you can separate yourself from what is present. Every automobile has at least three mirrors that are strategically placed. They all have a different function and allow you to safely maneuver through traffic at any given time.

The blind spot can get you into an accident if you are not careful, and this reveals to me that we must be aware of ourselves at all times. We must be in tune with our emotional health as well as our spiritual health. Some Christians think that they should be exempt from trouble and are often surprised when uncomfortable things occur. I am here to tell you that there are some things you cannot prepare for, but we should also be grounded so our foundation is not destroyed.

Blind spots can push you forward or they can set you back, but the response is a choice. I can remember in my early development as a young church musician, I was afforded the opportunity to play for the church my father pastored. I literally learned how to play in church during what used to be called devotional service. This was when any person in the congregation would strike up a song in any given key and I had to pick it up.

There were some keys I could play in better than others; but to perfect my gift, I had to learn how to play in all of the white keys as well as the black ones! You have to be a keyboardist to know what I mean! This process was baptism by fire on any given Sunday, but I was up to the task. Was I perfect? No, but I was determined to perfect my musical ability.

I became more curious about the Hammond organ and was intrigued by the sound and how different it was from the piano. My music teacher at that time indicated that I had to master the piano before I could advance to the Hammond organ. I had to learn the rudiments which are the basics of playing the piano.

Before you can advance and move forward, you must look out for the blind spots of moving too fast! Don't despise what you deem as small beginnings, but perfect your natural gifts which will affect how your spiritual gifts will operate and you will gain valuable experience.

You must also be aware of emotional blind spots you may experience while your gift is in development. I experienced emotional blind spots as a young developing musician in the church and did not know how to respond immediately.

I was blindsided on a Sunday morning by being asked to remove myself from the piano because someone else was hired to do my job without prior notice. This was one of the most embarrassing occurrences that I had ever experienced. I had to get myself together and not make a scene while

39

maintaining my composure in front of the entire congregation. That whole day was emotionally draining and caused me to question my ability.

This blind spot caused me to re-evaluate where I was in my development and what to do next. I could have quit and not touched a piano, but I used this period in my life to get better and improve my skills. As I continued to work on my craft, I was granted other opportunities to use my natural gift of music. Work on yourself and identify areas of growth. Your areas of growth will cause you to be aware of potential blind spots as well as developing good vision.

I was blessed and fortunate to be given another opportunity at a neighboring ministry as well as my brother's growing ministry. God will strategically place people in your life to help you get to your next level of development during the transitions in your life. Don't overlook anyone because you don't believe they can add value to your life and development. Instead, embrace every situation as an opportunity to grow and make progress!

I was not as experienced as my mother and other musicians in our church community at that time, but I wanted to emulate some of the styles I was exposed to. I used my blind spots to help me to improve my musical gift while developing character. This experience taught me how to respond to people as well as develop my leadership skills.

I had to go through my experience to help me get to the next level by being pushed out of my comfort zone. You cannot become comfortable with what you have but begin to pursue better for your life.

Another blind spot is dealing with your vulnerabilities. We tend to view vulnerabilities as negatives, but they actually keep us aware of our limitations and what is within our scope. It's not that we limit ourselves but there are things that we are predisposed to that we must use to our advantage. You may have a specific handicap or you may not be experienced in a certain area. This just means that you have to work harder to get your desired results.

There will be seasons in your life when you will have to evaluate your skillset and learn how to respond to difficulty as well as opposition. While I was dealing with the downturn of the real estate market, I had to deal with my own vulnerability relating to how I would move forward and earn an income for my household. It took me a while to realize that I had a choice of staying where I was or do something different!

I made the decision that I would jump into another aspect of sales where I could use my talents as well as gaining a new license. There will be times when you may not like the options that are presented to you, but make a determination to do something. I used my time away from real estate as a means towards an end. I knew if I kept working and moving forward that my season would change and it did!

Despite the blind spots you may encounter, find a way to press forward! I encourage you not to quit because you have hit a brick wall. Instead, find a way to get passed it! I promise you, if you keep going and find creative ways to get to a place of restoration, you will discover that there is more in you than you think. Be resilient!

Action Plan:

1. Get in tune with your health and the well-being of your body by scheduling annual check-ups.

2. Don't make a rash decision but ponder the after-affects.

3. Maintain your composure during tough experiences.

CHAPTER 8

USE WHAT YOU GOT!

"A man's gift maketh room for him, and bringeth him before great men." Proverbs 18:16 (KJV)

What you have inside of you is valuable! I believe that it is essential to use your natural gifts; and if you are a Christian, you have at least one spiritual gift. Whatever you were born with must be developed and over time, it will manifest if you allow it to come to life.

In my experience, if you are able to do something with limited effort, this is an area that is usually tied to your natural gifting. This does not mean that it is perfect but it will be perfected when you exercise it and put it into use.

I was born into a musical family which consists of some who are vocally gifted and some who can play multiple instruments. I was not interested in much as an adolescent and had difficulty finding my way. My mother was instrumental in identifying my musical gift and did everything necessary to help me develop it by finding a piano instructor for me to take piano lessons.

No one could give me the gift but it had to be cultivated, and I also had to practice daily. Anytime I went to my piano lesson and did not practice the week before, my instructor could tell immediately! She would notice if I followed her instructions and directives.

People cannot make you do anything, but you must have a desire to become better at whatever gift

43

that resides within you. This idea applies to the potential that is within you. You possess it now but you must extract it. What things inside of you need to be manifested?

Using what you got requires time and effort as well as knowing what your gifts are. Sometimes other people will identify things that exist within you but this should be a confirmation of what already exists inside of you. It is simple to take the easy way out. But not using what you have may delay your progress and it may take longer than expected. Remain committed!

The process of development and maturity may be quicker for others but you cannot allow yourself to be frustrated by what you deem as little or no progress. You must not be trapped by competing with other gifted individuals. You must learn how to be comfortable in your own skin and use your God given ability.

Competition can be useful but it should be exercised carefully. Believe it or not, competition exists in the church at large and it extends into the secular community and the work place as well as family.

People are trying to gain a competitive edge in life. You must find a balance and be clear in what you are designed to do. Many people are trying to outdo each other because of what they deem as success. Determine your own success by using what is inside of you.

You can be successful at your own pace by using your gifts to empower others while it is being developed. This was the case for me when I was an up and coming musician. Every opportunity I had to play the piano was an opportunity to exercise my natural gift, learning how to lead others, perfecting my musical gift, and edifying the congregation.

From time to time, other experienced musicians would fellowship with our congregation and I gleaned what I could by listening and watching what they did. Was I trying to be competitive? Yes, but I was also aware of my skill level and stayed in my lane. This routine can also work for you in your place of employment, as an entrepreneur, or your profession. Seek out those who are successful in the area that you strive to emulate. Ask questions, seek advice and counsel, find out what their routines are and you will experience changes that will take your life to another dimension.

Stay in your strategic lane and develop your gift. Keep practicing, take classes, earn a degree, and by all means - keep learning! Before you know it, your gift will take you to places you would not have imagined.

ACTION PLAN:

1. Use your natural gift(s) to enhance your spiritual gift(s).

2. Cultivate your gifts and talents!

3. Engage in healthy competition.

4. Use your gifts to enhance your life and the lives of others!

CHAPTER 9

STRATEGIC VISION

"Then the Lord answered me and said: "Write the vision and make it plain on tablets, that he may run who reads it." Habakkuk 2:2 (NKJV)

Having strategic vision is a necessary component in life, ministry or applicable vocation. I would advise anyone, but especially those who are in high school, to begin to think about their life and what they would like to do upon graduation. It is not too early to begin laying the ground work and establishing a plan. If you don't plan now, you will fail later or delay your productivity.

After graduating from high school, it was my intention to possibly go into the service and travel the world. I never told anyone about this until now. I passed the ASVAB which is the initial test to go into the military, but something strange happened. I had a change of heart and decided to go to community college. This was actually the best decision that I made as a young adult.

Attending college is not for everyone but I encourage all young adults to do something after graduation. For me, college seemed to be a better fit and it allowed me to stay close to my aging parents. Interestingly enough, my dad had a stroke in the fall of my first year of college. I had a plan but God had another one! Staying at home and going to college afforded me the opportunity to help around the house and to develop my musical and leadership skills. These two areas have been the foundation of who I am today.

My strategic vision changed as I attended college while growing into young adulthood. Your life trajectory and strategic vision can change due to circumstances beyond your control. It really comes down to how you will respond and the direction you will ascend.

As I continued college, my major changed multiple times until I just gave up! I decided I would find full-time employment and just work. This was a crucial time because I also rediscovered other gifting's that I was blessed with, as well as a call to be a minister in the Lord's church.

What we deem as a waste of time could be the building block of God's plan for our life. I later discovered every class I took was beneficial to my development, and I did not lose any credits when I transferred to Washington Bible College which is now known as Lancaster Bible College.

You must be able to see yourself differently and be aware of things that may be hazardous as well as being flexible. Flexibility includes being willing to change and adapt. Having strategic vision for your life will demand a great investment! The size of your investment will determine the outcome and your withdrawal.

You must be able to navigate clutter and roadblocks and not have tunnel vision. There will be times when you need to have tunnel vision. I will speak about tunnel vision later in this chapter.

You must be willing to employ strategic vision for your life by gleaning from successful people. I was blessed to have many examples of those whom I deemed to be successful by putting my thoughts into action.

Strategic vision allows you to see beyond your current reality and the belief that better is coming! Strategic vision will allow you to find strength when you are at the lowest point in your life. Strategic vision will also allow you to see the motives of people and what role they will play while on your journey. Everyone is not against you. There are people who God will place in your life to help you and they will be a strategic part of your process.

Tunnel vision can be viewed as a positive or negative characteristic. I believe you should use tunnel vision to focus on opportunities that will guide you towards success while ignoring obvious hindrances. By now you should realize that everyone will have distractions but tunnel vision will help you focus on the outcome and not the problem and look for solutions.

I previously mentioned that we have to be aware of clutter and navigating roadblocks. This has the potential to kill your dreams and suppress your potential. How do you avoid it? I suggest that you create physical and mental space. If you are one who has a lot of clutter at home, you may not be as organized as you could be. Take time to throw away anything that is not beneficial to your life. Regarding mental space, take time to meditate on God's word as well as find helpful resources that will point you in the right direction.

ACTION PLAN:

1. Think about your life in strategic segments and start planning for the future. (Have a 5-year and 10-year plan)

2. Navigate your roadblocks with strategic vision.

3. Look for solutions and do not focus on the problem.

4. Be flexible!

Chapter 10

Putting It All Together!

"I can do all this through him who gives me strength." Philippians 4:13 (NIV)

As we come to the close of this journey, now is your time to put the pieces together. As with any puzzle, it will take time but it will be worth every moment that you are willing to make the commitment.

It took me a considerable amount of time to get to the place that I am in today. I invested time and energy in things that were profitable and helped me financially as well as educationally.

I had to remind myself that my past failure was not final but it was the conduit that has fueled me into a new season. Don't beat yourself up because something did not work in the manner you thought it would. Get up and try it again!

Your peers may seem to be making more progress than you, but don't be distracted! Remain focused on your race! Take all of what seems like broken pieces and use them to get back to a place of stability.

Don't waste time by doing nothing! Take action that will bring success to your life and you will be blessed. Not only will you experience fulfillment but those who are connected to you will benefit because of your decisions.

Move strategically towards your successful life. Success comes one step at a time, so get moving! Take action that will bring restoration and healing to your life and I promise that your life will be better because you decided to make a move! Make a move toward becoming a better you and pass it on! You can do this!

ACTION PLAN:

1. Make a commitment to yourself, research thoroughly, write your plan(s), and don't be afraid to fail!

2. Remember progress is progress!

3. Use your mind and discernment to assist you to make wise and smart decisions.

STRATEGIC MOVES

www.ingramcontent.com/pod-product-compliance
Lightning Source LLC
Chambersburg PA
CBHW060201070426
42447CB00033B/2253